SNOOPY

(features as)

Man's Best Friend

Charles M. Schulz

Printed and bound in Great Britain
for Ravette Publishing Limited,
Unit 3, Tristar Centre,
Star Road, Partridge Green,
West Sussex RH13 8RA
by Cox & Wyman Ltd, Reading, Berkshire

ISBN: 1 84161 066 6

PEANUTS

7-18

SUPPERTIME ISN'T FOR ANOTHER HALF HOUR

I WAS JUST HOPING FOR A FEW CELERY STICKS...

HOW ABOUT THAT? I WALKED ALL THE WAY OUT HERE WITH YOUR SUPPER DISH BALANCED ON MY HEAD!

5-18

THIS IS WHAT HAPPENS WHEN YOU EAT IN THE SAME PLACE EVERY NIGHT!

I DID WHAT YOU WANTED... I CALLED THE HUMANE SOCIETY AGAIN

THEY SAID THEIR BUDGET WON'T ALLOW THEM TO GIVE OUT FREE RAINCOATS TO EVERY DOG AND BIRD IN THE COUNTRY...

EVERY TIME THERE'S A GOOD SUGGESTION, SOMEONE BRINGS UP THE BUDGET!

LUCY SAID WE SHOULD DO MORE THINGS TOGETHER

SHE SAID IT MIGHT HELP ME TO GET OVER FEELING DEPRESSED..

1-26

I THOUGHT MAYBE YOU'D PLAY A GAME OF CHECKERS WITH ME..

I SUPPOSE I HAVE TO LET HIM WIN, TOO...

© 1983 United Feature Syndicate, Inc.

5-20

SERVICE!

THAT'S NICE, BUT IT ISN'T EXACTLY WHAT I MEANT...

NOPE, YOU WERE WRONG

THERE I WAS, SLEEPING PEACEFULLY...ALL OF A SUDDEN, I THOUGHT I HEARD A HUNDRED-VOICE CHOCOLATE CHIP COOKIE CHOIR CALLING ME...

I WONDER HOW I COULD HAVE BEEN WRONG ABOUT A THING LIKE THAT..

9-29

SEE? "ACE SLEEP DISORDERS CENTER."... THEY CAN TEST YOU, SIR, TO FIND OUT IF YOU HAVE NARCOLEPSY...

WELL, I'M SURE NOT GOING ALONE! IF SOMEBODY WENT WITH ME, IT MIGHT NOT BE SO BAD...

IF YOU CAN FIND SOMEBODY ELSE AROUND HERE WHO FALLS ASLEEP ALL THE TIME, THEN I'LL GO...

9-14

© 1983 United Feature Syndicate, Inc.   9-13

HELLO, CHARLES? I'M CALLING TO TELL YOU ABOUT YOUR DOG

9-15

SNOOPY AND PEPPERMINT PATTY HAVE GONE TO A "SLEEP DISORDERS CENTER"... WHY? TO BE TESTED FOR "NARCOLEPSY"

THEY KEEP FALLING ASLEEP ALL THE TIME

IS THERE A CENTER FOR SOMEONE WHO FEELS HE NEVER KNOWS WHAT'S GOING ON?

GUESS WHAT..I'VE BEEN ASKED TO BE IN THE CHRISTMAS PLAY!

I'M GOING TO BE AN ANGEL

12-15

© 1983 United Feature Syndicate, Inc.

ALL I HAVE TO DO IS SAY, "HARK!"

I'M GLAD THEY DIDN'T ASK ME.. I WOULD HAVE SAID, "BARK!"

YES, MA'AM, HE WANTS TO RETURN THIS BOOK HE GOT FOR CHRISTMAS

HE DOESN'T LIKE IT BECAUSE THE HERO IS A CAT...

HE HATES CATS

BLEAH!

HE WANTS A BOOK WHERE ALL THE CATS GET EATEN BY ALLIGATORS ON THE FIRST PAGE!

Other PEANUTS titles published by Ravette ...

Snoopy Pocket Books

Snoopy features as ...	ISBN	Price
Master of the Fairways	1 84161 067 4	£2.99
The Fitness Fanatic	1 84161 029 1	£2.99
The Flying Ace	1 84161 027 5	£2.99
The Great Philosopher	1 84161 064 X	£2.99
The Legal Beagle	1 84161 065 8	£2.99
The Literary Ace	1 84161 026 7	£2.99
The Matchmaker	1 84161 028 3	£2.99

Snoopy's Laughter and Learning series
wipe clean pages
(a fun series of story and activity books for preschool
and infant school children)

Book 1 - Read with Snoopy	1 84161 016 X	£2.50
Book 2 - Write with Snoopy	1 84161 017 8	£2.50
Book 3 - Count with Snoopy	1 84161 018 6	£2.50
Book 4 - Colour with Snoopy	1 84161 019 4	£2.50

PEANUTS Anniversary Treasury
(224 pages featuring some of Charlie Brown's favourite
strips in colour and black & white)

	1 84161 021 6	£9.99

You Really Don't Look 50 Charlie Brown
(over 500 daily and Sunday strips and a series of
Charles Schulz essays celebrating the anniversary year)

	1 84161 020 8	£7.99

Prices are subject to change without prior notice.

All PEANUTS™ books are available from your local bookshop or from the address below. Just tick the titles required and send the form with your payment to:-

BBCS, P.O. Box 941, Kingston upon Hull HU1 3YQ
24-hr telephone credit card line 01482 224626

Prices and availability are subject to change without prior notice.

Please enclose a cheque or postal order made payable to BBCS to the value of the cover price of the book and allow the following for postage and packing:-

UK & BFPO:	£1.95 (weight up to 1kg)		3-day delivery
	£2.95 (weight over 1kg up to 20kg)		3-day delivery
	£4.95 (weight up to 20kg)		next day delivery
EU & Eire:	Surface Mail:	£2.50 for first book & £1.50 for subsequent books	
	Airmail:	£4.00 for first book & £2.50 for subsequent books	
USA:	Surface Mail:	£4.50 for first book & £2.50 for subsequent books	
	Airmail:	£7.50 for first book & £3.50 for subsequent books	
Rest of the World:	Surface Mail:	£6.00 for first book & £3.50 for subsequent books	
	Airmail:	£10.00 for first book & £4.50 for subsequent books	

Name: ....

Address: ....

....

....

Cards accepted: Visa, Mastercard, Switch, Delta, American Express

Expiry date .... Signature ....